POEMS

WRITTEN FOR

SBEK'S MUMMIES, MARIE MENKEN, AND

OTHER IMPORTANT

PERSONS, PLACES & THINGS

by

ANNE PAOLUCCI

With an Introduction
by GLAUCO CAMBON

TO MY MOTHER, LUCY

ACKNOWLEDGEMENTS: I wish to thank the following publications for permission to include in this collection poems which have already appeared in print: *Kenyon Review* for "Fathers Day"; *Literature East and West* for "Fragments from the Chinese Classics" and "Dream of the Eastern Chamber"; *Quicksilver* for "Poetry Reading" and "Little Boy Brown"; *Balsam's Ass* for portions of "The Time of the Great Horn" and "Survey II"; *Anon* for "Big Doll"; *Forum Italicum* for "To Sylvia" and "The Calm After the Storm" (both slightly revised); *Italian Americana* for "Duets in Three-Quarter Time"; *Poem* for "Hyperbole," "To Gemini," "To My Mermaids," "Emblems," "To F.W. in Search of his Mask."

Library of Congress Catalog Card Number: 76-53263
ISBN: 0-918680-03-4

Designed by Iris Papazian
Manufactured in the United States of America

GRIFFON HOUSE PUBLICATIONS
H. Prim Co. ● 38 West Main Street
Bergenfield, New Jersey ● 07621

CONTENTS

What a delightful surprise. I should have suspected long ago that Anne Paolucci was a poet, though I knew her only as a brilliant scholar and critic; but she isn't the kind of litterateur who indulges in total and instant self-advertising. The sheaf of poems Anne has now shown me affords a privileged glance into that deeper part of her mercurial self which she normally hides from the world where she seems so much at ease, and of course it bears the imprint of considerable craftsmanship.

Quibbling about the relative degree of success and failure in each poem is not my concern at this point. What matters is the presence of breakthrough, not its omnipresence. And while the case to be made for Anne Paolucci's verse rests on that intermittently but unmistakably achieved breakthrough rather than on inevitable "perfection," much is to be gained by paying attention to the versatility of her voice, a voice which easily moves through a variety of registers, from the witty to the grave, from the colloquial to the tersely lyrical, from the elegiac to the self-deflating and the satirical. She likes to put on masks: Sbek in the Egyptian vault, Cleopatra with Egypt at her breast, Galla Placidia in her alabaster chamber; a variation on Pound's personae? But then she probes beyond, or rather behind, the mask; and the imaged grandeur crumbles under a ferocious scrutiny which sets up a progession of inverted grandeur, as in "Notes on Still-Life":

> . . .*Or take plants instead.*
> *Stun them into giants,*
> *Give them the look of murder,*
> *Paint them dead.*
> *Or words. Under the hard touch*
> *Of type, sow with full hands,*
> *Wait for turds*
> *To lure flies.*
> *Maybe that's best.*
>
> *There's looking into mirrors too.*
> *You can try that, when you're ready.*

This is one of the breakthroughs I was talking about, where sweet Anne, civil Anne, sophisticated Anne, comes to grips with the horror of reality. That horror challenges even the last safeguard, the act of writing, "poetry." One can use literary ability as an alibi to avoid or defer such a confrontation, as if one could say, "Yes, reality is sometimes horrible, but since I can translate it into artful words, I am superior and remote." That's when mirrors come in handy.

The persona looking into so destructive a mirror is the Anne I did not know before reading these pages. Instead of a shock of recognition, I experienced a shock of unknowing. I felt like asking: "Who are you, Anne?" But that is the question she has been asking herself, or else she could not have written what we are reading now. And that telluric Anne has the right to fling the disturbing question back to me, to us; and unless we expect the poet (the woman poet at that) to be unfailingly gracious and abdicate savagery at all costs, we shall do well to heed the question. "Poetry is a destructive force," said Wallace Stevens. How much easier would it have been to say that poetry is a creative force. But listen to the consequences, in Anne Paolucci's case, "on reaching the age at which [her] father died":

> *Stranger than God,*
> *Infinitely awesome,*
> *Your young dead face,*
> *Stern hands folded limp*
> *Over a cruel sleep;*
> *And the child now withered in me*
> *Like a guilty thing*
> *Reaches down into a wide stillness. . . . .*

The destructive force that is poetry demands to be exercised and, at times, personified, why not, into "Apollo"; and then

> *His demon lover watches*
> *Over him*
> *Contrite but firm,*
> *Brooding on the block of marble*
> *From which the destroyer*
> *Waits to be chiselled.*

I can imagine Rilke as an interested reader of this poem; and Rilke again would have listened to the sharply contracted music of "Kuki," in which the numinous power of things, their mana-like *thingness*, is released:

> *Candles, tables,*
> *Amber vases change*
> *Shape, sing their*
> *Terror on plaster and*
> *Brick. I almost wept*
> *Trimming the wick.*

Once the poet has looked into the Hades that lurks beneath the familiar surface of things, her eyes will be cursed with painful clairvoyance affording, as Melville would put it, sharp probings into the axis of reality. But the poet, the poetry, cannot subsist for very long on such perilous threshholds, and from them there will be a necessary retreat into the more familiar world, where Anne's voice can attain resilient modulations—particularly when she remembers an Italian country childhood, Roman-campagna style, in "Acuto," or fancies what her alternative life would have been "back in the old country" if she had chosen (or been allowed) to remain there:

> *Back in the old country, a white beaver coat*
> *Would be presumptuous, even in a dream;*
> *I'd dress in black or in a cotton print*
> *And bless the Lord for a warm shawl*
> *On Sunday. . . .*

I love the intonation here, and the ability to see and understand and care, after some potentially destructive knowledge. The Italian counterpart to these texts (three in all) is linguistically flawless but somehow it's the English that holds me; and perhaps one should read the subsequent bone-dry pieces like "To Clare" or "Sunday Dinner" against just such a nostalgic background, hell present versus paradise lost:

> *. . .All this comes back*
> *As you knead dough*
> *In an over-heated kitchen*

This flour-sprinkled morning.
Hell is this feast of flies.

And with this, we are back to the bitter truths of the first poem quoted above. Anne is not always the dark, terrifying "Anne" I have been trying to exemplify, nor is she always as strong or as supple; but—since I have mentioned her bilingual skill—I feel obliged to single out her translations from Leopardi (a telling choice) for special praise. Leopardi, a poet of bitterness and despair who knew what sweetness could be, is not easy to translate; but Anne Paolucci has found such persuasive approximations, such elegant interpretations for "To Silvia" and "The Calm after the Storm" that in her rendition they sound like English poems to begin with. Translation is a gift, like poetry itself; and like poetry, a long patience. More power to you, Anne.

GLAUCO CAMBON
March, 1977

DREAM OF THE EASTERN CHAMBER

I. SBEK'S MUMMIES

There was a time, said Sbek
With a smile (I could not tell
If boding good or ill), when luck
Truly served me well--

The Fayum sleeping still
Under the pharaohs' dust, lions
Stalking the desert, the Sphinx
Barely half-awake, my mummies
Quiet in their sacred shrouds.

I would walk up and down
Between the rows, taking notes
All day. At sunset Becker
Would drop by to drive me back.

That Spring, at Khartoum,
We met Gordon. The three
Of us played chess at night
Smoking and sipping scotch--

And then the mummies began to stir.
You know the rest.
Poor Gordon stood his ground
But in the end the Mahdi
Claimed his head. Becker
Soon after disappeared.

What could I do? I moved in here,
Arranged with Beboulth, my guide,
To bring in food. Still
The mummies will not rest.

All day this buzzing
Like fever pressing on the ears
Like vultures swooping down
To see if I still breathe.

What could I do? I gave Beboulth
My books to take to Cairo;
Another would take care of me
(I said) while he was gone.

But, already you have stayed too long.
Go now, before the moon sets
And the lions come. Say you left Sbek
With his mummies
In Thothmy's tomb.

II. MAYA

Move as the Indians do,
Slowly.
Scratchy surfaces catch
Dreams, pluck them loose.
Move with the dead
Gracefully.
Mourners veiled in light
Following our noon-day tracks
Without looking back.

Don't stop. Don't hurry.

The gods choose as they please
When they will.
Move quietly
As though it did not matter.

NOTES ON STILL-LIFE

At night, bridges pick up their fat legs
And move through muck and water
To shore. I know. I've seen them.

Headless giants, they congregate
On grass by the highway
And call on Oedipus
(Patron of swollen feet)
For deliverance.
Never mind golden birds
Grecian urns
Busts of emperors.
This is better.

Try willing it. What do you see?
Daily rape. Monsters clutching
That huge spread
Rushing toward orgasm
On sudden ramps,
Coming to rest in driveways
And garages.

Or take plants instead.
Stun them into giants,
Give them the look of murder,
Paint them dead.
Or words. Under the hard touch
Of type, sow with full hands,
Wait for turds

To lure flies.
Maybe that's best.

There's looking into mirrors too.
You can try that, when you're ready.

TO MY MERMAIDS

Nancy, my darling,
And Brishkai, and lovely dark-haired temptress
Whom I christen, precious in sadness,
Melancolia,
Should you some morning
Put aside confident divinity,
Stand naked stripped of saris,
Love's flowing perfection
In whose faith you are infinitely beautiful,
I will take you to quiet coves
Where gods pass through in the guise
Of clerks and shopkeepers—
They will lure you of course,
And one of you will surely stay behind!
And those who turn back
Will suffer questions that cannot be answered,
Cleopatras, each with a new Egypt at her breast.

ON FIRST SEEING THE BLACK GRANITE
STATUE OF NJEGOŠ—POET, BISHOP, KING

I held back an ironic smile
Crossing the empty lot
To the shed (planks loose,
Splintered, halved,
Black with rain, caked with mud,
The whole tilted slightly
To one side), where—
My hosts explained—
A special treat awaited me.
I watched them work the lock
Thinking ahead to lunch and drinks,
Mumbled something to their apologies
—The spring was rusty, would not give.

I should have known they had already
Scored many times before;
When the door at last creaked open
Shock strangled my impatience
Melted rising laughter in my bowels.
Massive, black, knees spread apart
Cradling his own bleak vision of *pietà*,
An eagle poised upon his back,
Mestrović looked out through Njegoš' eyes,
Shattering the sun with dark surprise.

I spoke, I know, some stupid thing,
And all the while I saw the statue
On its mountain top, the lonely seer

Shaping the night into a new Olympus—
And gripped by something almost fear
I turned my face
From that awesome presence still at rest,
Stepped back and looked away
Until the rusty lock was back in place.

SPEAKING OF HAMLET—

God-maker every one of us,
Shapers of trinities,
Every fondness baked in clay
According to our fancy
Which changes every day.

That kind of love survives
Do-it-yourself divinities—
What artist do you know
Will slash his own pictures?
What sculptor break his venus?
What writer burn his books?
It's easier, good lord! to bury children
With a dirty look.

ENTRANCES/EXITS

Why do eunochs come to mind?
Voyeurs without the saving grace of lust,
Whose bodies are love's ruins,
They open and shut doors for Semiramis
(The sullen temple cat in us all
Following her prey with fierce eyes)—
That's one kind, one door.

A glance has its entrance
And its curtain call,
And, sometimes,
The wounded god
Uncertain of his role
Traces the contours of the soul
The cave's dimensions,
Shadows on the wall,
Measures the stone floor,
Opens floodgates.

Beyond Dionysian/Apollonian masks
Winter sweeps all seasons to their rest.

CLAMS WAITING FOR DIGGERS
ON THE BEACH

The tide goes out
Trailing its belly
A little further through sand.
Entrails of dead fish,
Loose seaweed, bottles, logs
Pile up on the strand.

At midnight visitors sing
On balconies over the bay,
Stare at the bridge
Where mirages sometimes
Walk cables, sit on top,
Plunge below feet first.

Later, the rush of the dead
Behind us,
We doze avoiding sleep,
Drown in wet clay
Daily explosions and retreats,
The pulse of our own breath,
Wake to reshape
A new image each new day.

Sometimes we see a stranger
Digging below,
Measure the length depth width
To which we grow.

MERIDIANS

Plato said
The wise must be forced to
    Become deans
    Teach freshmen courses
    Advise honors students
    Demonstrate and take on government jobs.
He was wise
Did none of these things
But there is truth in what he said.

Aristotle, a faculty of one,
Tutored Alexander
(Who died at thirty three)
Collected plants
Researched dissertations
—There is truth here too.

Augustine, avant-garde teacher
Of his day
Gave up fame, still young,
To consider larger issues
Mold his own contemporaries
Advise generals
Write books.

St. Francis (patron of hippies)
Was a volunteer in hospitals
In underprivileged areas
Led leper marches.

And poets, of course—
But they were all banned
In the greater cause,
And to some that too is
Illumination.
Still—Plato exalted them
Aristotle explained them
Augustine brooded and wept over them
St. Francis, inspired, joined the group.

Shall we do less
In our rigor for nice distinctions?

ITE

Some paint their mirrors kind,
Some—like Brutus on the hill—
Stab badly.
Some live out wrinkles
Cut deep around smiles
But turn quickly
From the shock of other eyes.

In the mind's mass
Startled into a guilty thing
I stumble to contrition
—Prematurely, it seems,
For no one there
Will listen.

FATHERS DAY

He was tired
Distempered and hungry
From the long dusty trek,
He did not know
It was Fathers Day.
He knew not the chariot
Stuck in the narrow path,
The horses foaming
Under the hard impatient
Blows, the old man's
Hot and tired curses.
And yet he was no stranger.

Later the corpse was dug up
The scars still fresh
Under the matted hair
And there the matter rests
Despite gold and incense scattered along
The road to the palace door,
Despite the banquet and the curious
Guests. In the long afternoon
Between the first curse and the last
There is time for a nap
In the sun-room, time
To digest and forget.

MATILDE'S SONG

Really be true to one another?
Lovers grow gently into golden birds
For emperors and lords
Who envy Cleopatra
And kill Antony with bread and cheese.

For, look you, my Lord—
Startled footsteps find Persephone
Sooner or later—
In the rubble of night
Between earth and bones
The ghost of Hamlet
Reaches up and clutches our flowing memories
Holding back judgment
Of wilted flowers, long silences,
As though it did not matter.

Or does it?
Lovers grow weary into poems
(Don't look back!)—
They mold beauty into truth,
Call it Good,
Clap hands, make music, dance, will not part,
And call it Art.

GALLA PLACIDIA IN HER TOMB

I sit here, Empress of Rome,
Sister and wife of kings,
Beloved of Aetius and Boniface;
Many struggled and fought for me,
Adored me, died for me
Each in his own way.

My life, now ended, waits
To be shaped again
Under this dome;
In regal robes I sit out
Solemn eternity staring
At green and white patches
Outside my home.

My glory and power preserved
In this temple of bricks,
I brood of trees and woods
Where once I paused, between
Hope and grandeur, to love.
Memory plays tricks
Despite my crown. I bore
Children, cradled their laughter
In my soul.

Saturn, forest on forest
Upon his brow,
Circles my dream of empire;
I too wore majesty with sadness,

Welcomed exile—
There is more to death
Than stolen fire.

READING OF THE SCROLLS

Coiled about signals
(The poet's traffic)
                    Light up
          Come
     Now laugh
   Go
Think hard
Spools spiraling toward silk
Smooth transparencies
(Shelley's Baia depths
Buried towers sapless ocean foliage)

Drown.

Uneasy the head under haiku crowns,
Buddha smirks listening to strangers
Filling time between busses
Shuttling them in and out of Spring
Through yellow country singed brown
Green fields speckled red
White nodding meadows sloping
To river-swift marriage in cool valleys—

Up and down come and go
Seasons of fools
Unraveling the poem.
Wind the clock goodnight
And curl up in an anapest
While dreams flit past

Pisa's Sirocco pines
Sink into a tired Mediterranean.

Zen prayers stir
Under the dirge of bells
Toll soft-remembered silences
To their shells.

FOOTNOTE 1

Lord, in the fog of Great Events,
In ruins of mysterious intentions
Largo to allegro
Our daily places made imperfect
(Who's that?)
Mirrors back to back,
Tell us how when where
To exit gracefully
Dissolve infinite reflections
On blank walls—
To drag it out,
Shout for lights,
Stretch smiles across our curtain call—
To step aside
Relinquishing Promethean fire,
Find some lesser stride—
One single moment will do,
Wings fluttering to air
Tracing a pattern on the wind,
Even a winter sun
And faded colors on a scrim.

TO GEMINI [WHO LURKS
A GUISA DI LEON CHE POSA]

There is the Holy Land.
Down the street behind Orange Julius
Is the hill
Daily crucifixion.
Oh, it rains too
But nothing washes off.

There are worse deaths, I suppose.
Like not stopping to "WAIT"
Or stopping but not wanting to,
Like "Excuse me" to cross-bearers,
Like drowning beer with wine.

We surface surely in some form—
Grief in Rock Creek,
Foreign hills where earth smells
Of age and rot
And donkeys lose their way
Over cobblestones,
Or windows that are Japanese panels
Or cats.

Or unexpiated death
Dragged through the bowels
Nailed to the back of eyes
Oozing deliverance
In measured groans

(Each a new knife
Twisting in the wound)—

Then gently, for mercy, but quickly too,
It catches and holds, deftly, at its tip,
The tongue's cry
Between breath and breath.

ON REACHING THE AGE AT
WHICH MY FATHER DIED

Years enough, yours, for lust,
Some war, children, pain ready to snap—
They rattle like pebbles
In the heart's cavity.

Stranger than God,
Infinitely awesome
Your young dead face,
Stern hands folded limp
Over a cruel sleep;

And the child now withered in me
Like a guilty thing
Reaches down into a wide stillness
To pluck suns
Uncorrupted kisses
Fresh tears.

The sound of the past
Over my shoulder
Is a familiar voice.

HOROSCOPES

Leos know long before the event
What must be. They take it in stride.
Alcestis, Antigone, Joan, the Annes of the world
(Those I know) are all compulsive and wise.

But if I had a choice,
Could shape my birth
Map my route all over again,
I would prefer to be Antony,
Achilles, Jesus, or Allah
For many reasons which
(Being a woman) I could never explain
To a man.

Handwriting
Bumps on the head
Stars and crosses in the right palm
The 600 rules of orthodox superstition
Are the threshhold of mystery.
Are you happy to stand
Leaning against the doorpost
Savoring the innocent delight
Of the uninitiate?

Leos would leap across
Or pull back and shut the door.

TO MY UNKNOWN GIRL

Rotten is ripe
Like avocados—
Still, to be firm again!
Prolonged just a little-little bit
With a bite-size question
Into the fruit of things.

She, the child, that very instant
Mirroring all tragedies of all Eves
Since the first love-making
Where leaves were shed,
Some day will stand at check-out counters
For beer and cheese and gum,
Glassy eyed
Be asked a question
By a friendly bear or a gazelle,
And stumble into a diamond-studded answer.

NEW BABYLON

Ripples, Cryder House,
Political dinners at the Waldorf
Where dancing vies with speeches—

Orgies of duty
Sway virtuous lovers
From their task.
What would you do
In my long-gowned commitment?

Would you come late
In gray tweeds and a Pucci
Sunburst (when everyone else
Is in black tie?)
Would you seek out friends
And reminisce about the last time,
When Great Public Figures
Graced the dais
Who since have been surprised
In their own secret concupiscence?

What I did,
I danced.

APOLLO

The hair is thin
And eyes focus
In a dim sort of greeting—
Still, it is a statue
I think of,
And all around
Living things shoot up
Crying attention.

And when the god sleeps
(Fitfully with secret fears)
His demon lover watches
Over him
Contrite but firm,
Brooding on the block of marble
From which the destroyer
Waits to be chiselled.

KUKI

Candles, tables,
Amber vases change
Shape, sing their
Terror on plaster and
Brick. I almost wept
Trimming the wick.

DUETS IN THREE-QUARTER TIME

ACUTO

Non credo mi ritroverei
Se non fosse per il monte
Incoronato dalla nebbia,
I suoni chiari del mattino,
L'asinello che vien
Tirando su per il vicoletto
Sotto la finestra.

Qui nella fredda luce
Di abitudine
Infilo i giorni
Spianando i nodi
Che tirano memorie incaute:
Il sole non arriva giù
Fin qui. Ma
Nel mattino incoronato
Di asinelli e carrette
Piene di mele fresche
Per mercato,
Saprò la strada:
Fanciulla
Attraversando di corsa
La piazza affaccendata,
Giù per il vicolo
Che dà nella campagna,

Giù passate le stalle
E le capanne, fino
Alla casa di mio padre.

ACUTO

I am afraid I shall not know
The place, unless it is
Mountains crowned in a mist,
Clean morning sounds,
And the friendly donkey
Struggling up the narrow path
Under my window.

Here in the cold light
Of habit I thread my days,
Smoothing the snags that catch
On inconsiderate memories:
The sun does not reach down
Deep enough here
For recognition. But
In the purple morning
Of Angel-donkeys carting
Fresh apples to market,
I shall know my way:
A child
Running across the busy square,
Down the path below
The open fields,
Past stalls and sheds
To my father's house.

SULLA PIAZZA

Sediamoci. Il sole cala
Sul tetto del Barone,
E le campane suonano
Ai vesperi le nonne stanche.
Ecco il fattore vien
Dalla campagna,
Stivali pien di fango,
Cappello largo, viso bruno
Che guarda e tace,
Un pò del signore nel passo
Lungo che suona sulla strada.
I vecchi sdentati salutano
Dal muro della piazza,
E dalle ombre del vicolo
Lo stridío del carrettone
Che torna dal mattino
Giù nei campi.

Quest'ora bruna fa ricordare
Altri vecchi, con bimbi
In mano, passeggiando
Sotto un cielo giovane,
Per strade piene degli odori
Della domenica. Allora
Avevo anch'io un vecchiarello
A chiamare dalla piazza
Mentre il giorno calava,
E le campane suonavano
Al lutto un'altro sole.

ON THE SQUARE

We'll sit a while. The sun
Is setting behind the Baron's house
And churchbells ring tired
Old women to vespers. Here comes
The overseer, back from the fields,
His boots all caked with mud,
A wide hat shadowing his face;
In silence he passes by, confidence
In every step that rings
Against the cobblestones.
Toothless old men greet him
From their place beside the wall;
From the shadows of the lane
Comes the rumble of a cart
Returning from its morning
In the fields.

This hour of dusk recalls
Other men with other children
By the hand, strolling
Under a young sky and savoring
Familiar Sunday smells.
I too once had an old man
To call home from the square
As the day set and churchbells
Rang to rest another sun.

NEL VECCHIO PAESE

Nel vecchio paese, un paltò di castoro
Sarebbe prepotenza, anche in sogno;
Vestirei in nero, o in un cotone stampato
E ringrazierei il Signore per la sciarpa
Calda di domenica. La sera siederei
Davanti al focolare, lavorando i ferri,
Ascoltando il raschiare di penne sui quaderni,
Mentre i ragazzi preparano le somme
Dei loro giorni, coniugano il passato
In due belle colonne, e sognano dell'avvenire.
Là, in quell'altro mondo, sarei forse
Campagnuola, cantando il mattino
Al suon della fontana, tornando a casa
La conca piena sul capo. Nel paese paterno
Bimbi in stracci mi fissano e le giovinette
Mi sorridono;
Con la mia gente, nella mia casetta,
Mi sento sicura— quasi non fossi venuta
Per una scappatina, da lontano,
Nel magnifico paltò di castoro,
Una straniera americana, con un che
Del Lazio nel viso, ed occhi pieni
Di nostalgia.

BACK IN THE OLD COUNTRY

Back in the old country, a white beaver coat
Would be presumptuous, even in a dream;
I'd dress in black or in a cotton print
And bless the Lord for a warm shawl
On Sunday. In the evening, I'd sit
By the fire, knitting caps and sweaters,
Listening to the scratch of pens
Over notepaper as the children add up
Their days, conjugate the past in two
Neat columns, and dream of the future.
Back in that other world, I might have been
A country girl, singing my mornings
To the fountain's tune, carrying a pail
Of water effortlessly on my head.
In my father's village, shabby urchins
Stare at me and young girls smile
As if they knew me. Among my people,
In my own place, I feel secure—as though
I had not come on a visit from afar
In a magnificent white beaver coat,
An American with a familiar kind of face
And a nostalgic look around the eyes.

TO CLARE

I see my niece coming up the walk,
A Botticelli-type, slender,
Full of light, some few pimples
Just behind the hair
Above her right ear.
"Don't pick," I tell her with a frown.

But she, moving in her own brand of grace,
Laughs at my words,
Knowing her power and her spell.
Eve masks her premonition
Flaunts her beauty
Waits for dark angels at noon.

I won't play God.
Besides, she'd never understand.
The laying on of hands
Must come and all too soon.

PLAY IT AGAIN, SAM!

Women knit
At guillotine spectaculars,
Rush for choice seats
In the gallery
Without apology.

Fallen idols deserve their fate,
Betrayers, are betrayed in turn,
Reap what they've earned.
Good show. The audience applauds.

Gladiators in Panasonic gore
Stumble into focus at the door
Sweat through each blow
The past swept at their feet
Into a composte heap.
Thumbs down for absolution
Fill the screen to execution.

Knitters gloat
Through layers of transcripts
Documents and notes;
Time binds and stores away the grudge
Once the deed is done
Full circle the point won.

The dead are willing victims
Step into shrouds on their own—
So much is true even under oath

For carriers and lepers both.

Truth is an adequation of the two—
Candy bars, TV crew,
Lunch breaks while standing on the queue,
Crusaders unraveling their sleep
To see what Nemesis will do.

Symbols change but formulas
Remain the same.
New circuses will come to town,
Other strippers, other clowns.

SUNDAY DINNER

We sat listening for signs
In the rustle of leaves
Flights of birds
Oracular against the sky.

From her holy precinct
The priestess eyed us
Where we sat
Quietly sewing buttons.

All this comes back
As you knead dough
In an over-heated kitchen
This flour-sprinkled morning.
Hell is this feast of flies.

FRONT ROW CENTER
[A "HAPPENING"]

All of us dream doomed heroes
In Homeric sins.
We clear empty spaces
Stubborn before long lines
Of Hecubas,
And the innocent in us
Clings to safety
As plumes in strange helmets
Trace monsters in the air.

Behind magnificent shields
On which our battles and glories
Are wrought in gold,
We steal up behind the
Hamlet in us
And free the secret sharer.

Isn't that what we wanted
All along?
A perfect script?

LITTLE BOY BROWN

Hot voices rise from crevices of night streets
From cracks in the black pot
Where curses thicken under
A well-fitted lid.

Be not afraid child
Of the stranger
Struggling to get in
Without bumping into things,
Struggling to get out
Without being seen.

Except for the moment of shame
Of invisible pain and terror
When turning he sees
Little boy brown wide sad eyes
Watching him,
He will not know—

He will not recognize
His own young face
Across black years,
He will not want to trace
The slow uncoiling of his fears.

BIG DOLL [For Marie Menken]

42

Had Dante found the BMT Marie
I think he would have come
Straight to your place,
Sit and gossip about Guido
Dylan Dorothy and the bearded boys
Who lay garlands at your door.

Willard would have entertained him
As befits his genius-friends who bask in
Idem manebat neque idem decebat
Rabelaisian warmth
With champagne punch (what else?)
Farfallian fare
Devilled shrimp and potted pigeon
Boursault Gewurtztrauminer
Flaming pudding Ciacco would have praised
From Hell's glutton kitchen—

They would have talked
About dearth of feeling
Pirouettes and solar-pulses
Morphinology and curls,
Charming the huge dogs
With images of stars ice sun girls
Stuffed birds in Adams cages,
Would have tried his wings
Hearing about angelic grubs
Turned butterflies.

Had Dante found the subway to your place,

He would have recognized
Little-girl-gold-tired shape
Hiding under taffetas and Sitwell shawls,
Would have stripped your buddhas
To their Lithuanian core,
Bared Sunday frescoes on your wall,
Smiling innocent sleep all the while
He would have tucked you
In your faith
Without a word.

PARTY OVERLOOKING THE NARROWS
[To Robert Lowell, who wasn't there]

At my age
A party is a routine sacrifice.
Incognito
I stand Olympian
In the midst of critics,
Hounds from printing houses,
Girls from Ohio
Learning how to live,
Professors stretching myopic egos
To the social test.
I wait for food
Wondering if editors
Have time to brood.

Miss Gotham
As delicate a bird-lady
As ever wore a flowered straw
Stands listening to bearded lore.
O beautiful young man,
What's love to birds,
To ladies raised on Schraffts?
Do they write poems
Sit on grass
Roll over on the lawn
Wait under umbrellas until dawn?

At my age
I'm just a peevish guest.

THE SYBIL'S SONG

Age has its laurels,
Enough at least to keep us in routine,
Feel comfortable in it
Secure
Wanted.
Confidence is quite another thing.

Those who wrestle with gods,
Rising from restless dreams
Days of agony
Nights of claustrophobic panic,
Stand on the thin shore and brood
About the dead fetus in us all—

Bareheaded, die grim
(Friends toast them
Across pleasant candlelight),
Tortured, go naked to their gloom,
Puppets in knowledge
That trees, more friendly,
Shed leaves for them,
Waters stir their bones,
And the sun, in sublime detachment,
Bleaches their love, mercifully,
To dust.
They have their reward.

And there's the poet in us all
Who flings himself with abandonment

Into the lion's den
(The vampire's nest,
Nightmare of the flesh),
And wakes us in a sweat.

SURVEY I

What's Heine to him?
The drone of my voice
Catching on halos
Is cheap silence
Compared to the soft echo
Of rain on new leaves,
The pressure of a mattress grave.

SURVEY II

48

Well, it's hard to explain.

When you reach
Deep and over craggy words
Your daydreams heavy hang in sleep,
Don't stop or
You'll wake dead
In your tracks.

It's hard to scan.

Oh yes, and shut the door,
That's hard. Creep back
Into cool mosses,
Tuck yourself
In.

KINGS FROM THE NORTH
(From THE TIME OF THE GREAT HORN)

In our Viking youth
We spearheaded the northern straits
Coming upon wild Saxon soil
Where suns lay at our feet
And nights were mild.

There were times when the best of us
Grew weary listening to strange gods
In the forests whispering
Among themselves.
Later, the trees were cut,
Dew gleamed on our spears,
In time, they blossomed.

Now, in our Gothic age,
We look back
To the northern straits and beyond
To a wild land crowned with snow.

They are not dreams for old men.
In the moonlight with ghosts
Of giant trees stirring in the ground
We sit in silence
Remembering rusty spears
Buried by the sea.

FRAGMENTS FROM THE CHINESE CLASSICS

I. From SPRING ANNALS OF THE
    EMPEROR'S HISTORIAN

King Ch'in sacrificed a black ox without
    blemish
For the birds were fair;
He offered exquisite jade
(I, unworthy one, record the gift);
The bones read well
For ploughing the sacred field.

King Ch'in in yellow robes
Sprinkled new seed according to the rites
    prescribed;
The *shih* was silent in his trance,
But reeds whispered and far away
A mighty wind uprooted giant trees;
The augurer warned against the Northern
    tribes
And hearing this the King went forth,
Fearless One, with twenty thousand men.

Coming back through swamps, Ch'in
(Great Conqueror of the Northern Tribes)
Grew sick and died. Thus ended T'ien,
As the augurer had prophesied.
After came the Hsi,
Now gloriously reigning Wang-Tzi-ti.

II. COMMENTARY OF MASTER LIU
In the twenty-seventh year of T'ien

King Chin died of fever in the swamps
Near Ch'u-ni. Fifteen years he reigned
And with his death
T'ien came to an untimely end.
Fu-tsi P'ien, the Dowager, proclaimed
    herself
Regent for the Prince
And made her lover Tang
Chief Minister.
One day, while hunting in his park,
Prince Yu was killed. Then
Tang gave Fu-tsi over to the palace guard
Who strangled her before his eyes.

Thus ended the dynasty of T'ien
(As the augurer had prophesied).
After came the Hsi,
Now gloriously reigning Wang-tzi-ti.

III. From THE BOOK OF ODES

The Yellow Ancestor spoke through Liu:
    Listen for wild geese
    In the second moon, for the tiger will
        come
    To the river's edge and drink blood.
The Yellow Ancestor spoke through Liu:
    Listen for the screeching of birds
    In the full moon, for the green dragon
    Will rise from the river and set fire to the
        fields.
The Yellow Ancestor spoke through Liu:
    Listen for the sound of hoofs and bells
    In the fifth night of the fifth moon.
    Then shall I come

To mourn the ghosts of T'ien
Scattered like petals before the mighty Hsi,
Now gloriously reigning
Wang-tzi-ti.

IV. THE VISIT TO K'UNG FU-TZU

Mo-chu asked: What must I do
If called to serve the Hsi?
—We are here to serve.
Tsi-Tsung asked: How shall we serve?
—Fix the rites and supervise
Exchange of goods.

Mo-chu asked: What must we do
If the Northern tribes attack?
—Resist all thought of war!
Tsi-Tsung asked: And if we fail?
—The Emperor must have missed some rite!

The visitor from Chao asked: How can we avoid
What is corrupt?
—Seek those who pause and listen.
Tsi-Tsung asked: Master, who is wiser,
Chung-Chu or Mo-chu?
—Ching-Chu knows the rites, can be trusted.
Mo-chu seeks perfection in goodness,
Should be loved.
The visitor from Chao asked: What is goodness?
—I cannot tell you (said the Master)
For I have not seen it in any man.
King Ch'in was kind and did not bear a grudge,
But he was not "Good."

Wang-tzi-ti is bold and brave, metes out
Just punishments and fair rewards,

But is not "Good."
Perhaps the Yellow Emperor was Good,
I cannot say.

The visitor from Chao waited
Until the Master had retired,
Then asked: What does it mean?
Mo-chu replied: What the Master said
Is like lotus petals coming to rest
On the threshhold. Soon
Shivering ghosts will crowd these steps
In expectation.

V. From TAO TE CHING

(LXXXIX)   Confucius once said:
"Words, Sir, are a hopeless trap
For unsuspecting fools;
This much I can tell you
Sitting here upon the holy mountain
With a white jade in my hand.
I have fasted seven nights and days
Waiting for Tao.
Your presence, Sir,
Is not exactly welcome.
Your shrill voice dragged me back
Just now to my flesh, unwilling guest.
I came back to say:
Put your words to rest
With these dead leaves and shavings
Of moonlight at your feet."

(LXL) "There is no Power outside of the
    Way;
There is no Way without Power."

Do not come closer, pray.
I cannot give you what you do not have,
I do not have what you think you want.
Keep your distance—
Though you utter no sound
I feel words knocking about
In that skull of yours
Like dry bones in a rattle;
I can hear the jangle of impatience
All around me.
Mind should be smooth as jade,
Still as the mirror of T'ien.
On it is carved this inscription
(But you cannot see it!)
"The Way is Power."
For you, my finely chiselled thought
Is nonsense.

I have not power to read your fate
(But I have Power);
Time is a seamless robe
Ill-fitting on one
Who regrets yesterday
Weaves hopes for tomorrow.
I have no way of telling
What you seek here,
No treasure to yield
To any who divined it not before.
What can an old man with whiskers
Bleached by long years

Give or say
To one who parcels out his life
In yellow silks and concubines,
Rites and shows?
We are T'ien apart—
I sit here, waiting for Tao;
You will hurry away carrying
These husks of words
To your chest of jade.

(LXLI) The Way is Truth, not books.
Not sages, not fasting, not fame.
Yes, I have found Truth
But make no further claim.
I cannot tell
What knocks about in this shell,
I will not speak
What I know.
Wandering in the spirit world
I have found Tao.
My soul peered out from its cocoon
And saw the curve of time
Circling the white lotus.

VI. From LI SAO

Swift, swift the river flows
Over rocks, between slopes of flowers,
Down to the sea.
Soft, soft the river sweeps
Through spring and autumn,
Moving between banks of trees.

The holy man in his hut
Hears the mournful stream
Fleeing from lovers.
The holy man in his silence
Hears the fury of the sea
Far-off as it leaps against the shore.

Swift, swift the coursers run
Into the battle-fray;
Cries stop the warriors' spears.
Soft, soft the women weep
Through spring and autumn,
Waiting on the river bank.

* * * * *

The walls of Lo-yang,
Sturdy and tall!
The walls of Lo-yang,
Proud and strong!

Young men and girls
Sing, dance;
Friends exchange
Exquisite verse.

The walls of Lo-yang
Sturdy and tall!
The walls of Lo-yang
Proud in their fall!

* * * * *

With the Han I went forth to conquer;
A young wife and child I left to weep.

Before me stretched the golden mountains;
Behind me, fields of yellow wheat.

With the Han I went forth to conquer;
A silent wife comes forth to welcome me.
Before us yellow mountains rise in the mist;
Behind us, a fresh grave roots me where I
    stand.

* * * * *

Turtle shells and yarrow stalks,
Birds and fire;
Who shall bring the news to the King?

The Crown Prince has fallen in battle,
His spirit walks across the land
In restless defeat.

Birds of death
Hover above the palace gate—
Who shall bring the news to the King?

* * * * *

In youth, hope warmed my dreams,
I longed for fame and came out fourth
On the *Chin Shih.*

In fatherhood, dreams unfurled my hopes;
I watched my son play under the elm
And wrote poems.

In disgrace, I hide the future
Like a piece of moth-eaten wool.

My son comes up to me smiling.
I smile back.

VIEW OF INFINITY
(A Translation of Giacomo Leopardi's *L'Infinito*)

This lonely hill was always dear to me,
And this hedge, which cuts off the far
Horizon on almost every side. But sitting
Here, gazing about me, my mind conceives
Limitless stretches beyond, silences
More than human, a calm so deep the heart
Almost shrinks in fear. And, as I listen
To the wind moan through these branches,
I find myself comparing its voice to that
Infinitude of silence; and the eternal
Comes to my mind, and with it all the dead
Seasons, and the present living one,
With all its sounds. Then in the very midst
Of this immensity, my mind drowns:
And sinking in this sea is, oh, so sweet.

ONCE MORE EAST

The Arab in me came and went
As I brooded sleep.
I found myself in David's tent
In one bold leap.

The Jew in me broke down and cried
Begged for rest.
They brought me to my bride
And bared her breast.

The Arab in me tip-toed back
As I closed my eyes.
The Jew in me peeped through the crack
And feigned surprise.

I woke, frost-bitten, in the morning sun,
Half-dreaming still—
Harems, belly dancers,
Kingdoms won—

My cat stared from the window sill
Uncircumcized barbarian
Measuring a bearded Arian.

POETRY READING

The gods are dead!
Long live the bearded Greeks
Bristling in their teeth,
Chewing crumbs lodged there
From Olympian feasts.

Doric legs prop up
The temple of words
Where silent worshippers adore.
The oracle has shut down
(From Delphi the news)
For an indeterminate time
While renovations go on.

How does one go about
Telling this to a full house?
Refund the money? Apologize?
How inconsiderate the dead can be
Leaving their masks behind
In the portico! It's all so confusing

Unless one follows celebrants
Each to his own garret,
Sees them eating peaches over the sink
At midnight.

FUGUE

(INSIDE LOOKING OUT)

A window opened on a strange court
Children-filled and fragrant
With young laughter.
The sky was a soft pillow of light.

In the room
Darkness crept out
Of corners, stretching
Long tendrils upon the floor,
Shrouding the dusty threshhold.

(OUTSIDE LOOKING IN)

Heaven is a kindergarten
Filled with small voices.
God, a child squatting
In the middle of the floor
Under a patch of light.

The men and women
Who watch,
Leaning on the windowsill
Looking in—
These are the damned.

[AGAIN] OUTSIDE LOOKING IN

Mind him, you said,
Reaching for wine,
Don't scratch the dead
Before their time.

Let the sun go down
Turn mouth to mouth
As the moon comes up
Turn gently south

Tip-toe back
To legs and thighs
Turn locks touch true
Where the morning bends
With a rush of blue

To peer into damp rooms
Mirrored galleries
After five
      before lunch
         between small favors.

TO F.W. IN SEARCH OF HIS MASK

Shall we be saved, transfigured in our dreams,
Each morning newly-fashioned out of sleep
To slip into crumpled magnificence?

Eyes focus on a hill of lights
(Water too in the distance)
Return to rest on chestnut trees
Outside the window.

Hands move east to west
Tension to tonic
Weaving smoke with the melodic,
Words break
Crash
Splinter
Roll under chairs,
Voices struggle for their place and pitch,
And there's no end without a script—

Only a rustling in the wings,
A sudden cue to stumble into the gods' own den
And suffer shapes according to their will.

SIX-FINGER EXERCISE

There's nothing wrong with Autumn—
The color's true, burnt out
In any form or shape,
A warning coming much too late
For those who have already
Turned their morning—

Green things carry bright suns
With them through rain and slush
Into a new Spring. They drive
Through their own mock death, smiling.
So much is true for leaves and men.
Both flutter to their rest
Still dreaming, curled
Around the edge of summer-time,
Settle quietly in age.
As it should be—
Crumbling into dust is mercy.

Unraveling, that's hard.
The flashing on and off kaleidoscopic,
When suddenly one day myopic images
Take on the look of Blobs
Or microscopic atoms seen through
The wrong end of a telescope—
That's another start, piercing.
Our own children grow fierce
Into enemies, stunt our love;
We will them into hell with us

(Our last hope)—
There is no purgatory for such shock,
No turning back the winter-clock,
No exorcist can soothe our haunted sleep—
We swing like Judas from bare trees,
Our eyes melting into rocks
Put there at the crowing of the cock.

PASSAGE AND VERSE

Body fears crowd body doors
(Fluttering of wings in holy places)
Small choirs sing deserted voices
Amber green toward golden presences—

At the gates of heaven
Another age, another Paul,
Might find some sort of alchemy
In the Fall.

LOOKING OUT AT MIDNIGHT

Once I was mad about Gershwin,
Curled my lips at schoolmates
Who shared the listening booth
With Beethoven.
          I'm embarrassed
Remembering! Still, it was no sin
(Acorns don't blush at becoming oaks)
And truly
The soul shook in the wonder of it.

Shall I one day look back
Dismayed at this lethargy
That has settled in?
The bridge outside
(Put there for guests)
Is a gaudy postcard,
And the sails and motor boats
Freighters and tankers
And one submarine that have traced
Infinite patterns on the
Waters of the bay
Are already polluted memories.
Beethoven has come and gone.

Who knows? In the soft
Core of being, where all faces find
Their single profile,
All things finally
Are superimposed on the master image,

Mozart and Krupa, Giotto and Warhol,
Ginsberg and the tender poet
Whose faith sustains me still,
Like shimmering leaves
Lacing the wind with metaphor,
First and last will blend, bend,
In the look of love.

HYPERBOLE

Like the Philosopher's magnet
That draws all things
To Him, forcing the heart
To His Bidding

The Lover turns the universe
Into longing. And that one point
In which all quiddity is transmuted
Into the image of the beloved
(Without choice, beyond scrutiny)
Is, like the comet's reach,
Impossible to plot.

No graph can chart
The certainty of that equation.

TO MY FAT FRIENDS

A simple theory, mine:
The soul in us
Circles in ever-widening orbit
Until drowsy, tipsy, tired,
It drowns.
Our puppet lines grow limp;
We raid the freezer then
For ice cream
Rip into pretzels
Potato chips
Watch Perry Mason
(The fat-idol of our waste),
By slow stages soothe our flesh.

Or, in Wordsworthian fare:
We brood first, refuse to eat,
Then all our energies burst through,
Find hooks, fly high, and spin
Around our youth!
Falling in love is but a passing feast,
The morning after tells us just how brief;
And when we glance behind
To apple cores and orange peels
Chewing gum wrappers, glad bags—
The history of our intentions—
We circle sleep to rest
In that point of no dimension
Where Satans burn their blessings.

LISTENING TO THE GOD'S SONG

Listening to the god's song
Was bleibet, aber stiften die Dichter
Mocking in my ear,
I reach clumsily
Into my bag of tricks.

A wild fox poised
In transubstantiation
Distracts me.

The stuffed bluejay
In its Chinese cage
Mercifully turns my purpose
Into sleep.

THE JUST

Why martyrdom?

Among a silent hostile race
Dark angels push me back,
White strangers stare me in the face,
Graceless in shock
Look judgment and thunder
Shout
Force me Black
To safety.

MAN OF THE HOUR: [*TIME* PROFILE]

Once he was all pimples
Sallow-tempered among ruddy faces
Grumpy with body cares
Self-conscious in familiar places.

From the sidelines
He watched Harvard men debate,
Learned to mingle
Sip champagne, make others wait.

Singled out
—Eagerly expected, always late—
He mastered politics and sex
(Who can resist the Platonic bait?)
Until there was no place for surly
Perfection to withdraw.

Sainthood is something else,
Comes early.

PLAYING GOD

Pinter
Williamson
Grand Union
Diggins & Rose
Tow trucks
Flashing yellow lights
Moving vans
Hurrying toward ramps
As I watch
Smug conqueror
From my ninth-floor terrace.

On my right
The Island traffic moves
Steady red (Eastbound)
White bulging eyes (Westbound)
In and out of curves.
Black chimneys sleep
Across the water on the left,
And the giant piles of the bridge
Like some half-formed Atlas
Stand attention.

On impulse, even God looks down
Once in a while—
A man and woman step
From the glare of "Ripples"
Into a secret place
Through trees—

Even the true God true Man
In each of us
Can't tell where or why or what
Unless we have been there
Or will have been
Or wish we were. . .
And recognition like divine radar
Rivets imagination to the spot.

SAFARI

Dancer reaching for the dance
Seer struggling for light
Poet combing inspiration
For something bright
     scan faces
     wound bodies
     retreat subdued
     touch fire
Stretched high over intention
Peer through convention
Track down jungles
For elephants and ghosts.

There are signs
     but stopping to read them
     is death.
Beasts block the road
     will not be frightened
     by honking
     or silver bullets.

The sun is fierce.
Night is full of eyes.
Behind us strangers lie in wait.
There is no path through the mountains up ahead.
Time stretches out
In clouds of dust.
Are we game?

OLD AGE

78

A settling in for winter
The slush inside
Distilled to transparency
By the fireside.

And when the sun startles
Not ours but another's age,
Scarecrows wake painlessly
To scattered straw
Melting ice.

TO A SUPERANNUATED TEEN-AGER

Poplars, silver and green
In the poet's dream,
Dehydrated Sophia Lorens
Unfashionably lean—

For some strange reason
The image shimmers gleams
In spite of innuendoes;
We rise to it with pleasure
Take the beat of heart and spleen,
Call it wit.
Beguiled into the art of it,
Fumble for a hit
End up in the pit.

It was a good pitch, I thought—
But arrogance will trip
When caught nibbling
At its own taut words.
Me—
I'd rather be Ali McGraw
(Why deny it?)
But then,
Like all efficient birds,
I'll pick up any straw.

THE FUNERAL [To Au. D.M.]

I measure impotent rage
Against the feeble pulse
Of living and dead
Mingling in obscene consummation—
Watch you stumble up the aisle
Not yet transfigured in your pain,
Search wildly for an
Impregnable stone
To roll across this day's tomb—
That and forgiveness
For not having the guts to say
"He is risen."

The dead are hidden from view.
The dying drag behind,
Bent over their new age.
Knitted caps warm their grief.
Outside, a gray morning
Finds relief.

JANUS TO HIS SECRET SHARER

Two-headed monster-gods,
Ambiguous oracles—
Surely there's an affinity!
Macbeth, Oedipus, Tiresias
Are carriers and victims,
Doubles doubled
In geometric progression.
Not cancer but God-complexes
Eat away the fringe of things
To sudden recognition
In a hostile stare.

Until then,
Anyone can laugh,
Throw crumbs, shatter domes
Into kaleidoscopic magnificence.
And when innards have been
Picked clean, we turn
To Paris (our undoing)
For reassurance—
Terminal cases who persist
In picking the soul's scabs
Like smoking through tubes
In diseased tracheae.

IN LIMBO

Poets come into their inheritance
Upside down right side up
Through the center of things
Clinging to Satan,
Climbing paradox on paradox
In a countryside reconstituted
By seismographic nature gone mad.

Silenus (that spoiler of revels)
Insists on inventory
Sets up hurdles
Notes the distance between levels
Before the gods—gracious in their pleasure—
Bestow one and the other gift
With careless measure,
Without warning choose their vessels,
Toss a coin for heads or tails,
And the poet is hurled
Into the season of his martyrdom
Bare, blind, wild, dumb,
Without armor.

CAMELLIAS

Leaving, there was no time to gloss the text.
I followed the sound of my own soul
Down quiet lanes
Cradling pink-white-red
Mysteries in dark leaves.
We saw an alligator finally
One foggy morning
At Wakulla, remember?
Weaved gently in and out of coves
In an old wooden boat
Listening to phantom birds
While lone mermaid strands
Caught the water's surface
In slow siren-dance
And clutched my breath—

And in the atrium where the covered pool
Waits for summer suns
And pine needles crowd through
Wire netting overhead,
We smiled before our own
Infinite reflection.
There was no time to be explicit—

At a distance, your bouquet
Of prize-winning fresh-cut flowers
Wither in perfection,
Precious cuttings
In another garden.

GIN MASS AT HAPPY TIME

84

Like all other rites, this too
Exceeds comprehension.
We genuflect over platitudes,
Open the mind's crypt,
Walk through our own darkness
Like Jews waiting for a sign.

In deserted catacombs
We map our small epic,
Chip away at crisp greetings,
Kneel for a moment
In the sanctuary
Ravaged by brief suns,
Glance uncertainly
Over our shoulder
For friendly faces.
Faded frescoes trace the stations
Of our secret places.

THE BROMPTON ORATORY
[For Cardinal Newman]

I really don't mind guitar masses—
For many reasons
Stand solidly behind them.
Still, habit is weak,
Makes slaves of us
Even in retreat.

Crucifixions are another thing!—
One does not have to practice
What is preached
To feel magnificently
Unfamiliar grief that struggles for release
As we sit in our own lake of fire
Behind fluted pillars
Just inside a London day
Which moves gently
Through wind and sun and rain.

Graciously, the dead Christ
Who stirs in me
As a new Mary reaches out
To touch his feet,
Changes into another face.
Paul must have heard cappella singing
When blindness struck and seared
All arguments to dust!

Listening to those voices of decay,
The Luther in me found his clay,

Molded life into an empty niche—
Surely quite enough
To warrant sainthood for aesthetic priests
Who treasure beauty for such simple feasts!

FOR WHOM?

In a large sense, for
Plato
Shakespeare
My cousin Lea
(Whom I love)
The Premier of Russia
(Whom I fear)
Henry Kissinger. . .
And in fairness
Nixon too
(I lie I am told
Shrinketh from man
And faceth God)
—So let the bell toll it
The way it is.

Greatness sometimes survives
Books
Reputation
Love—
When all is said, I wonder,
Will an eternity of damp earth
Make up the difference?
Surely the dead must rave
Smelling the rot of flowers
On their grave.

ANTI-POLLUTION DRIVE

Bluefish, I am told,
Have come back deep into the Sound
To feed on tiny fish
Spawned in clear waters;
Rats feast on packaged garbage
Now that incinerators
Have closed down;
Housewives are being converted
To innocuous detergents;
Corpses may one day soon shoot up
In rocket-caskets to the moon
Or circle *cloaca maxima* a gilded sky.

There is a moral in this, surely,
Somewhere a happy ending to the story,
A perfect cure.

Someday, the last L & M
Will find its way
Into the Smithsonian
With all the other pleasures
Adam and Eve salvaged
From their Eden,
Where love suffocates among
The ruins of sex,
Its sick breath
Closing fetid on our addiction,
Fingers probing sticky nerve-ends
For perverse illusions.

The smell of orgiastic morning-after
Is still a plague inside our lungs—
I don't know that the pill
Is quite the answer—
Even those happy few
Who manage to survive
No-birth and no-control
Must struggle upstream through
Floods of swollen concupiscence,
Smog and sewers, jungle fevers,
Grow fangs, lure tigers from their cages.
Even the saved draw blood
Drink toasts and offer sacrifice
To daily lust.

PLATO'S CAVE

Those shadows you see
On the wall
Are the sun's words
The child's joy.
We creep to the threshhold
Pick up shining pebbles
In the sand.

There must be more.
Water washes things to shore—
Empty bottles, shells,
Sometimes the ocean's roar.

DAY OF RECKONING

If, as the poet says,
We shall one day
All be contemporaries,
Why brood?
If that nameless power
Which tempted our attempt
Is to be trusted,
Divine puppets will receive
Blank checks.
This too is faith,
Invisible music,
Strength.

Having resigned ourselves
To bland diets,
We yield, after a slight pause,
To pleasant indulgence.
The magic hand of chance
Is the poet's grace,
But standing in some dark corner
Of Westminster,
Even he must let go.

THE DEAD HAWK

92

Proud against the sea's
Battering breath,
Indignity is washed ashore.
Children creep up to stare
While bolder things
Crowd the unexpected feast
Try sweet taste of rotting sand
Clotted light.

Which is more cruel—
The mystery that plucked it loose
Or children gathered round?

EXPLICATION

Sympathy like patience
Is a paradox
Hard to come by.
Self-negation is heroic,
Not many have it.
Some feel its power
(Aesthetic at best)
—*Ricordati di me che son la Pia!*—
Write articles about it.
Sometimes, in dreams, we recognize it.

And when we wake,
In kindness hands reach out
For faces behind scrims,
Eyes scan props for wings.
Our daily world seems gideons away
In the midst of Spock galaxies.
Sad ghosts armored against our fears,
Materialize in and out of presence
Full circle to target
At will.
In dim deliberation
At dawn, we are still.

Who is the Mover? Who the Moved?
Behind the one glance
Defining each his past,
Words turn to butterflies
Settle in the stomach—

Letters, judgments, arguments
Suddenly are adequate.

ANAGOGICAL READING

Shall I tell you what I really think?
Well, then, Ravenna.
Large eyes luring us
Into empty corners
In stripped churches
Where mosaics walk
In a dazzling circle of air.

Not enough?
Herculanum. Pompeii.
Black dogs on mysterious leashes
Smelling out strangers
Twenty centuries away.
Persephone, face averted,
Leads to terracotta mysteries
Caked blue and green.

We follow, don't we?
Or we sleep in such memories
And wake to frayed curtains—

I'd rather be a ghost
Walking stone streets
Of buried cities.

ON THE EVE OF THE DUBROVNIK FESTIVAL

We walked through empty cloisters
Wired for sound
Where Delius was scheduled
To be performed,
Peered over tenth-century walls
Where Antonys—giant spots
Stalking them across the parapet—
Would fall;
Later, a gallery of paintings,
Quickly old manuscripts, icons.

Crisp, in low shoes, Buba mapped
The mini-tour,
Straining the clock, saw it through;
At noon excused herself for the day
(A family commitment!)
Having taken most efficient care
To find another host.
Just as well! I brooded;
Women, over-zealous, betray their sex,
Like fallen angels, boast uprooted,
Grow cold, still charming
Turn to stone.
It was unfair, perhaps,
But instinct leads us into traps.

Bosko picked us up for dinner
And scored at once;
We basked in his confidence.

In perfect stride, he painted canvases
With every word.
Men are beautiful, I noted,
When they can sit and listen, too:
Just enough female in them
To bristle, laugh, and wound us
Gently in our pride.

I envied Buba, scrutinized her shoes;
Loved Bosko, every wrinkle in his suit.
Judgment was absolute, without appeal.
Over coffee in a deserted bar
Late into the night,
While Buba somewhere was toasting
Her newlyweds with wine,
Bosko blocked his scene
And cast the roles for his own
Cunning play. Like spectators
Strung in and out
Of some cathartic vision,
We listened, awed, and thought
The artistry was ours.

Curtains must fall and actors disappear
Before we gravitate to touch
Thaw to recognition
Settle into paradox and definition.
Major and minor work up
To symphonic climax
Easily when art is mastered.
Midnight chords reach down
Into the early hours,
Strain familiar sound

For the sun's position—

In concert, step by step,
Through waiting halls and theaters,
I tuned my voice and joined the trio.

PEOPLE, PLACES, AND OTHER NIGHTMARES

Deep in the tiger's continent
(Lovers tracking me to discovery)
I turned breathless into the path
Of my familiar morning,
Makeshift drapes struggled
To keep the jungle sun
From peeping through broken blinds
In my bedroom.

I seized the light,
But something leaped out with me
From the dark,
Stretched its measure high and low
In wide-arched breath
Like an angry cat.
I whistled through breakfast,
By turns defied and spurred
My resolution. One must be fair
Assessing one's own standard size,
Unforgivable is to indulge in lies,
Steer judgment to our cozy slip
Back to back, self to self.

I wondered all through lunch
What sleep it was
That dumped its carcass
Across the state line between
Dust and dreams. I fumbled
In corners for the key,

Found the gate, peered out.

Clock-down fizzed away the day;
I rushed to a clearing out of bounds;
Even as I looked around
Something stirred behind my eyes,
Some other shape
Beyond the prism of my flesh.
It slipped into a pitch
Which no one dragging shadows
Can ever hope to reach,
Lured me to hallowed wastes.

I follow, like Enobarbus,
A thin sound struggling in the earth,
Look back to sleep. My own wild fear
Runs past and leaps into my bowels
As night rolls over me
Its huge birth.

ON THE ROAD TO DAMASCUS

Nothing's rosy all the way.
Glasses chip, mouths twist,
Lovers turn to gray.
In that limbo mist
Where all things fall in disarray
And God checks out his little list,
Our lusts will cool,
Cameras will move in close
To register the fool
Turned king in all his gross
Conceit; set rascals up to rule
Their betters with a dose
Of their own brand of pity.

Coming together in that final city,
Rebels and saints may grow witty.

ON READING HEGEL'S *PHENOMENOLOGY*

Sandwiched in between
Coming and going
We shape our habits
To their battered use.
The eye takes in
The giant screen outside,
Turning the scene casually
Upside down
Through a point of no dimension,
Restructures millenia of lines
On a tabula rasa
Already molded to receive
Molten fires.
Such images survive the mystery
Of conception;
Crossing wires is child's play.
The miracle is not death or birth
But history.

MEDITATIONS ON A BLACK TEXT

Some petty ruler surely lived
And died in grace,
Content with small gifts. . .
The daily pleasures of his race. . . .
He signed traffic bills
And rarely showed his face—
The details must remain a mystery,
They sink beneath the weight of history.

Sin casts heroic shadows
Even in disgrace,
Borgias and Saviors measure
With wide-arched daring the world's pace,
Overtake their age
Leap over rank and place.
Talents buried in the ground
Are gross incompetence when all around
Things surface through the earth and
      multiply.
Nature's ambition ripens sun and sky,
Scatters seed and turns the acorn into lie.

In sheep's clothing, the lion and the fox
Indulge in paradox—
The jungle forces them to claim
Their victory, stalk their game,
Move restlessly through fame,
Until the last bright death
When small and large pretensions
Take their stand

Between sun and sun
While others hold their breath—
What reckless judgment can be found
    to blame
Dead Majesty, who lies in shame,
Or Gonerils who nimbly seize command?

TO SYLVIA
(A Translation of Giacomo Leopardi's
A SILVIA)

Sylvia, do you remember
That time in your life on earth
When beauty shone
In your quick and laughing eyes
And—thoughtful, brimming with joy—
You climbed the peak of youth?

The quiet rooms,
The streets below
Rang with your flowing song
As you bent over chores
Dreaming of the happy future
Pictured in your mind.
May was in full bloom
Then, and thus you spent
Your days.

Sometimes, I'd push aside
My books—
Those soiled and wasted pages
Where my freshest years,
The best of me,
Were wearing thin—
Turn to the sound
Of your voice high above
The terraces of my father's house,
Your swift hand

Across the heavy loom.
I'd stare at the open sky,
At golden streets and orchards,
The sea off in the distance,
The hill nearby—
No mortal tongue can possibly describe
What I felt inside.

What lovely dreams!
What strength and hopes
My Sylvia! Life and fate
Seemed, oh, so different
To us then!
As I gaze back
On all that hope
A desolate and bitter grief
Takes hold of me, plunges me
Deep in mourning for my own
Wretched state.
Why, O Nature! Why do you
Keep from us the gifts you promise?
Why do you deceive
Your children so?

Before winter had set in,
Long before the grass had withered,
You died, sweet tender girl—
Worn out, destroyed,
By some disease deep down inside.
You never got to see
The flowering of your years,
Never felt your heart quicken
To sweet words inspired

By your dark lovely hair,
Your shy faithful glances
Full of longing;
Your pretty little friends
Never got to gossip with you
On Sundays, about love.

My own sweet hope died, too,
Soon after; my years, also,
Were denied their youth.
How dim, dear friend of my
Young age—my long-mourned Hope—
You now appear!
Is this that happy world?
—The joys, love, tasks,
Events we used to dream about?
Is this what lies in store for us?
When Truth rose up
You fell, poor wasted thing,
And pointed with your hand
To cold death
And a bare grave
In the distance.

THE CALM AFTER THE STORM
(A Translation of Giacomo Leopardi's
La quiete dopo la tempesta)

The storm is over.
I hear birds chattering and the hen
Ventures out again,
Resumes her cackle. Here comes
The bright sky breaking in the west,
On the mountainside.
The land is swept clear
And in the valley the river reappears.
All hearts grow light,
From every corner, the familiar hum
Of daily chores resumes.
The carpenter, singing, comes
To the threshhold, work in hand,
To gaze up at the misty sky;
The little housemaid
Steps outside, uncertainly, at the sound
Of fresh rain running past;
The herb vendor takes up
His cry along the street.
Here comes the sun again, smiling
Over fields and houses. Inside,
Balconies and terraces are thrown wide,
And from the drenched street
The sound of tinkling far-off bells,
The creaking coach, tells us
The traveler is on his way again.
All hearts are light.

Is life more tempting, sweeter,
Than it is right now
When each of us returns to books,
Resumes his tasks,
Begins new works?
When worries seem buried
In the past? --
Pleasure? Child of pain!
A vain joy growing out of ancient fear,
From which death rose to terrify
Those of us who'd learned to despise life;
In their long agony
—Silent, cold, pale with fright—
Men shook, broke out in sweat,
As clouds, thunderbolts, and winds
Were hurled against their sins.

O gracious Nature! Are these your gifts!!?
These the delights you offer us??!!
Delight is to be free of pain;
Pain you sow with lavish hand;
Grief shoots up next, of its own accord,
And if by some miracle, some freak of chance,
A bit of pleasure springs
From our suffering
That is great gain, indeed! Dear to the gods??!
Why, we are happy if spared some small sorrow;
And blessed is he whom death heals
Of every sorrow.

EPILOGUE

Satan, in his lake of brimstone,
Found his Socratic truth—
Why can't you?
One to one is the world's way,
Outside there is desert
And prayer. Which is it?

Some kind of flame rises in us
Stops us in our tracks
Consumes our flesh
Makes us cowards.
Like Oedipus, we choose our choice
And run away from self-made oracles
Until, in empty corridors,
We put on Kafka glasses
And say goodbye.

AT THE PODIUM

It's all the same,
Whether I speak in riddles
Or play the game,
Sit on the dais
Or out there
With the other guests.

Art is arrogance
And must be blessed
In public places
To survive its own grim trial.

Those who turn down such a test
Mask simply another kind of guile.

TWENTY-ONE JEWEL MOVEMENT

Face and hands ticktock
The revolution of our shocks,
Bright to dim we creep to midnight
Where the sun is still.
In-between, bare trees
Set off alarms,
And blinded by its own reflection
The will sometimes turns
Our daily trance full circle
With a single glance.

We hurry day to dust
Through gray landscapes
Bringing up the past.
The measured distance coiled
Inside the heart
Must run its clock
Before the final crowing of the cock.

ICARUS: A FLUTTERING OF WINGS

Smite sight, smash sound,
Overrule objections
To orgiastic sessions
Full of flack,
Mouth tracing dully back
Some hidden inspiration
To diluted presences
(Not quite ours but inviting
Nonetheless).

The ground moves beneath our joy
Like water beds,
Each flutter of stale breath vying
With visions of our secret dying
And waves cover up again
The sin of faith.
Short of virgin springs,
Cool banks, stoic bridges
Straining with the weight
Of concrete, our flying
Is all vaudeville,
Feet first.

[EPITAPH]

HERE LIE
PEACE MAKERS   WRECKERS
DREAMERS   ARCHITECTS OF GRAVES
POETS OF SILENCE   DEALERS IN WORMS

A GRIFFON—HOUSE PUBLICATION

H. PRIM CO., INC.   38 W. MAIN STREET
BERGENFIELD, N. J. 07621